# Letterland

Workbook 2 Level 1

## My name is

.................................................................

## Let's learn about...

j v w x y z q

vowels     blends     review

Fix-it Phonics

# Focus on sound

Find the objects starting with Jumping Jim's sound. Then colour the picture.

jam    jet    juice

# Focus on sound

Draw lines from Jumping Jim to the things that start with his sound. Circle the one that doesn't.

Draw something that starts with Jumping Jim's sound.

# Focus on shape

Let's write Jumping Jim's letter shape.

# Focus on shape

Let's write both his letter shapes.

**Jumping Jim**

Jj   Jj   Jj   Jj

5

# Focus on shape

Circle the one that is different.

Can you find Jumping Jim hidden in these words? The first words have been done for you.

Jumping Jim can juggle jugs.

Jim can do jigsaws.

Jim enjoys jam sandwiches.

Bye bye, Jumping Jim.

# Focus on sound

Find the objects starting with Vicky Violet's sound. Then colour the picture.

vegetables

vet

van

# Focus on shape

Draw lines from Vicky Violet to the things that start with her sound. Circle the one that doesn't.

Draw something that starts with Vicky Violet's sound.

# Focus on shape

Let's write Vicky Violet's letter shape.

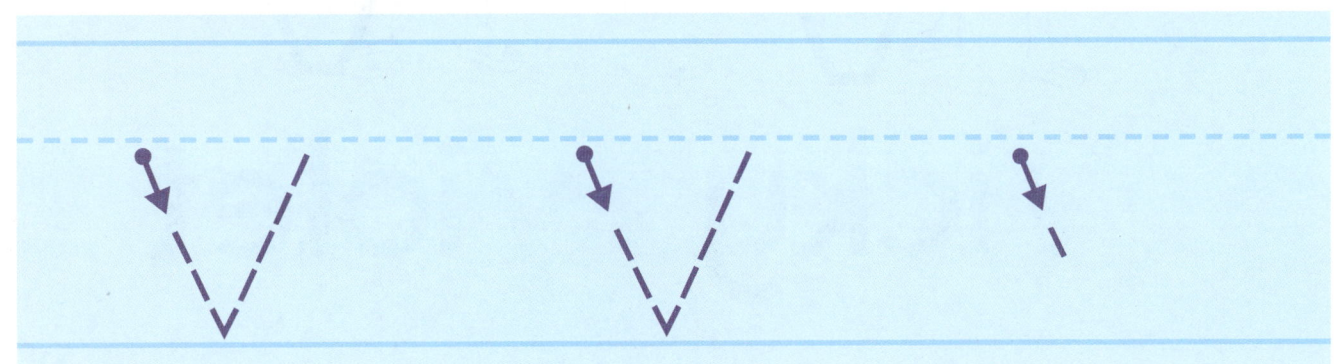

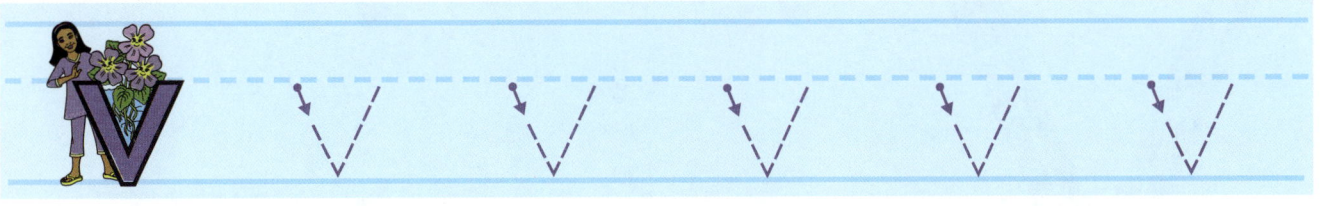

# Focus on shape

Let's write both her letter shapes.

Vicky   Violet

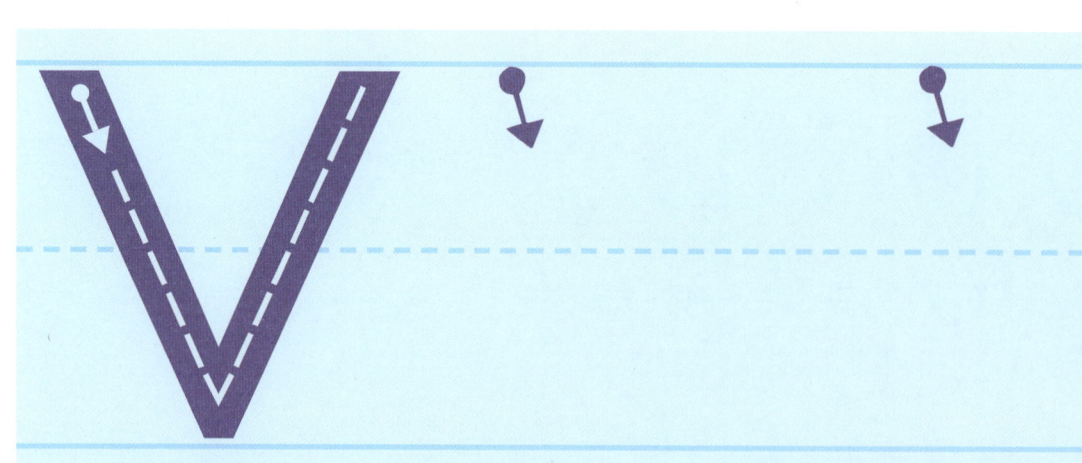

 **Focus on shape**

Circle the one that is different.

Can you find Vicky Violet hidden in these words? The first words have been done for you.

Vicky Violet plays the violin.

Vicky drives a violet van.

Vicky loves vegetables.

Goodbye, Vicky Violet.

# Focus on sound

Find the objects starting with Walter Walrus's sound. Then colour the picture.

water        watch        window

# Focus on sound

Draw lines from Walter Walrus to the things that start with his sound. Circle the one that doesn't.

Draw something that starts with Walter Walrus's sound.

# Focus on shape

Let's write Walter Walrus's letter shape.

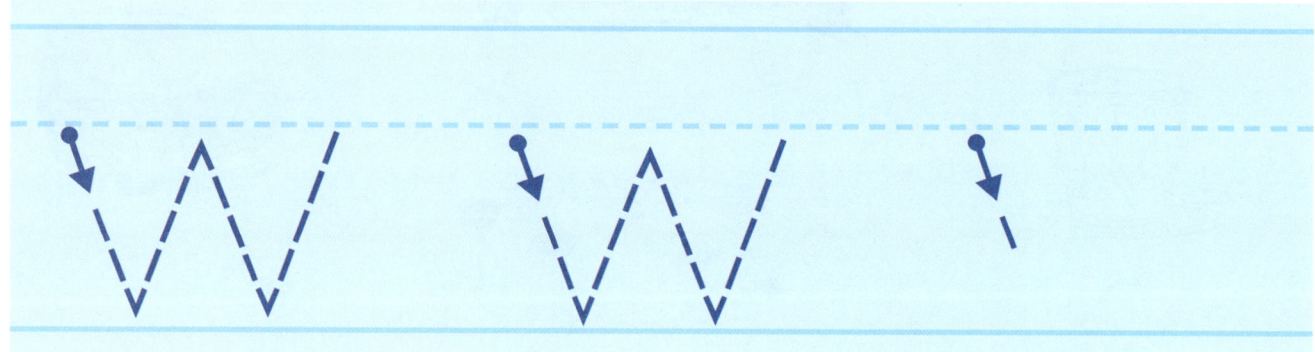

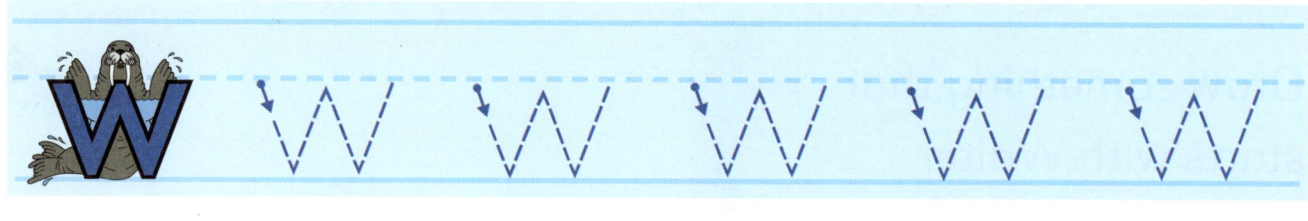

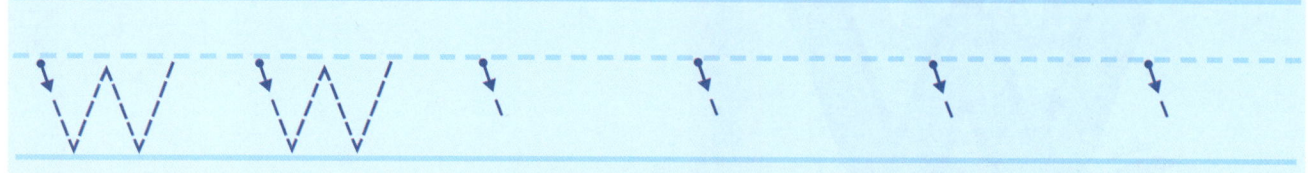

# Focus on shape

Let's write both his letter shapes.

Walter  Walrus

Ww  Ww  Ww

 # Focus on shape

Circle the one that is different.

Can you find Walter Walrus hidden in these words? The first words have been done for you.

Welcome, Walter Walrus.

Walter likes windy weather.

Walter is waving at you!

Bye bye, Walter Walrus.

# Focus on sound

Find the objects ending with Fix-it Max's sound.
Then colour the picture.

six    box    fox

# Focus on sound

Draw lines from Fix-it Max to the things that end with his sound. Circle the one that doesn't.

Draw something that has an 'x' sound in it.

# Focus on shape

Let's write Fix-it Max's letter shape.

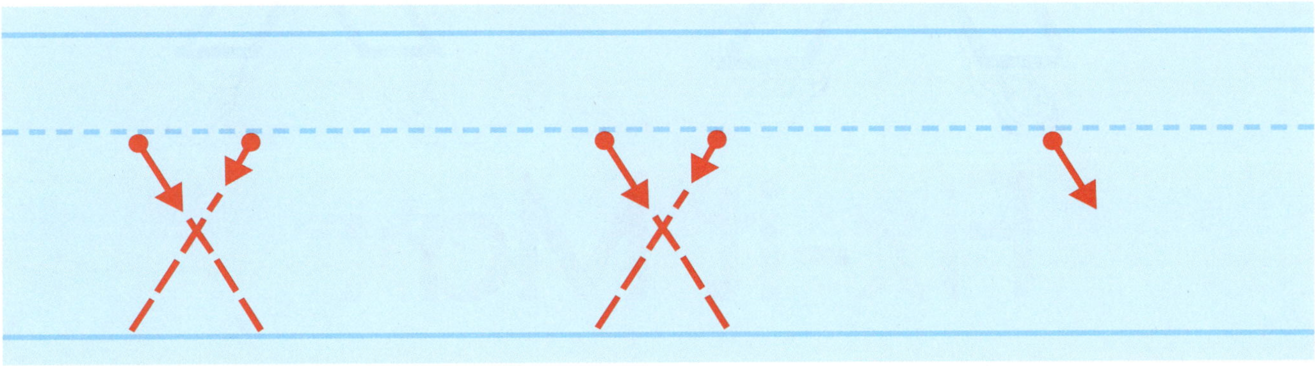

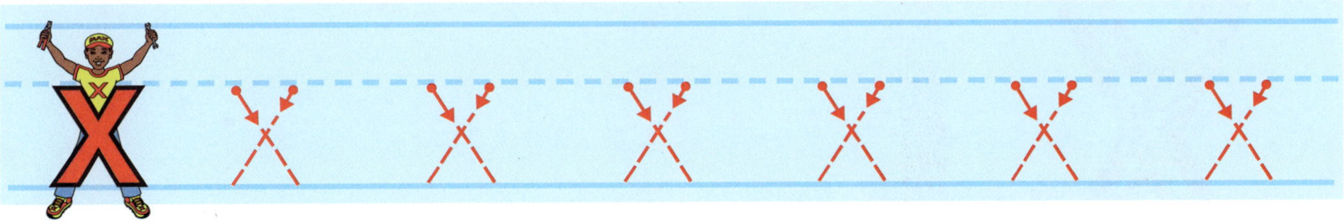

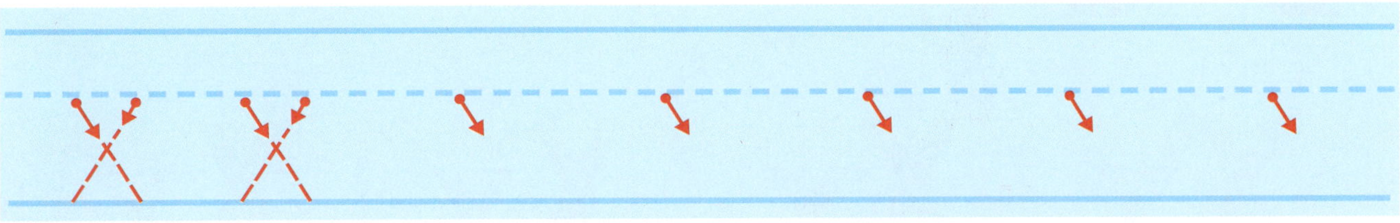

# Focus on shape

Let's write both his letter shapes.

## Fix-it Max

 **Focus on shape**

Circle the one that is different.

Can you find Fix-it Max hidden in these words? The first words have been done for you.

Fix-it Max likes exercise.

Max is six years old.

Max can fix things.

See you later, Fix-it Max.

 **Let's review**

Fill in the correct letters to make the words below.

j  v  w  x

bo_

_an

_am

_eb

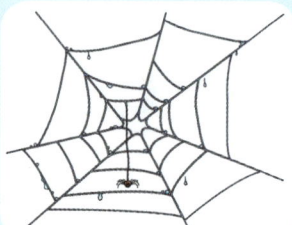

# Phonic Word Builder

Draw lines to match the words to the pictures.

**van**

**box**

**jet**

**jam**

**web**

Now can you write this whole word?

_ _ _ _ _

23

# Focus on sound

Find the objects starting with Yellow Yo-yo Man's sound. Then colour the picture.

yo-yo 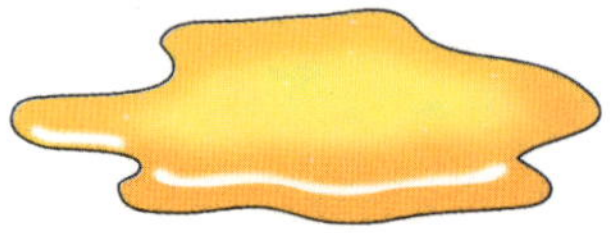         yellow          yogurt

# Focus on sound

Draw lines from Yellow Yo-yo Man to the things that start with his sound. Circle the one that doesn't.

Draw something that starts with Yellow Yo-yo Man's sound.

25

# Focus on shape

Let's write Yellow Yo-yo Man's letter shape.

# Focus on shape

Let's write both his letter shapes.

## Yellow Yo-yo Man

# Focus on shape

Circle the one that is different.

Can you find Yellow Yo-yo Man hidden in these words? The first words have been done for you.

## This is Yellow Yo-yo Man.

## Yo-yo Man's yogurt.

## Yo-yo Man likes yellow.

## See you, Yellow Yo-yo Man.

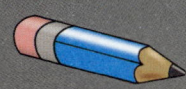
# Focus on sound

Find the objects starting with Zig Zag Zebra's sound.
Then colour the picture.

 zip

 zoo

 zero

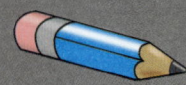
# Focus on sound

Draw lines from Zig Zag Zebra to the things that start with her sound. Circle the one that doesn't.

Draw something that starts with Zig Zag Zebra's sound.

# Focus on shape

Let's write Zig Zag Zebra's letter shape.

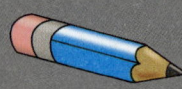 # Focus on shape

Let's write both her letter shapes.

Zig Zag Zebra

Zz Zz Zz Zz

# Focus on shape

Circle the one that is different.

Can you find Zig Zag Zebra hidden in these words? The first words have been done for you.

## Here is Zig Zag Zebra.

## Zig Zag lives at the zoo.

## Zig Zag's bag has a zip.

## Goodbye, Zig Zag Zebra.

 **Focus on shape**

Sometimes, Zig Zag Zebra's best friend helps him to make words. She is called Zoe Zebra.

# Zoe Zebra

 Zz Zz Zz Zz Zz

Can you find Zig Zag and Zoe hidden in these words? The first words have been done for you.

## The lemonade is fizzy.

## The bee says, buzz.

## Whizz! The boy is dizzy.

34

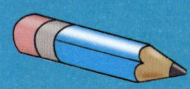
# Focus on sound

Find the objects starting with Quarrelsome Queen's sound. Then colour the picture.

question     quilt     quarter

# Focus on sound

Draw lines from Quarrelsome Queen to the things that start with her sound. Circle the one that doesn't.

Draw something that starts with Quarrelsome Queen's sound.

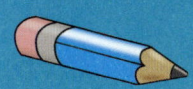

# Focus on shape

Let's write Quarrelsome Queen's letter shape.

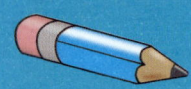

# Focus on shape

Let's write both her letter shapes.

Quarrelsome Queen

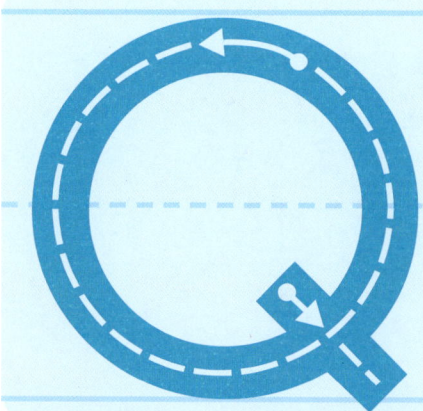

Qq Qq Qq Qq

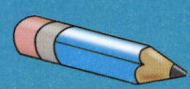
## Focus on shape

Circle the one that is different.

Can you find Quarrelsome Queen hidden in these words? The first words have been done for you.

Hello, Quarrelsome Queen.

Quiet, Quarrelsome Queen!

Quarrelsome Queen's quilt.

Bye, Quarrelsome Queen.

39

# Let's review

Fill in the correct letters to make the words below.

y  z  zz  q

fi___

___ip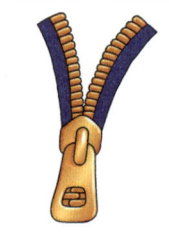

___uilt

___ak

# Phonic Word Builder

Draw lines to match the words to the pictures.

zoo

yak

zip

quilt

fizz

Now can you write this whole word?

c  k

# Focus on sound

Write the first letter in each of these words.

 says 'a...' in  ant.

 says 'b...' in bed.

 says 'c...' in cat.

 says 'd...' in dog.

 says 'e...' in egg.

 says 'f...' in frog.

# Focus on sound

Write the first letter in each of these words.

 says '**g**...' in **grass.**

 says '**h**...' in **hat.**

 says '**i**...' in **ink.**

 says '**j**...' in **jam.**

 says '**k**...' in **king.**

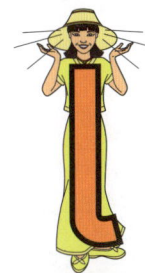 says '**l**...' in **log.**

# Focus on sound

Write the first letter in each of these words.

 says 'm...' in

 says 'n...' in nine.

 says 'o...' in on.

 says 'p...' in pen.

 says 'q...' in quilt.

 says 'r...' in run.

 says 's...' in sun.

# Focus on sound

Write the missing letter in each of these words.

 says 't...' in  ten. 10

 says 'u...' in 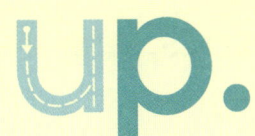 up.

 says 'v...' in van.

 says 'w...' in wind.

 says 'x...' in  fox.

 says 'y...' in yak.

 says 'z...' in zip.

# Focus on shape

Practise writing all the vowels below.

Annie Apple says, **a a a**.

Eddy Elephant says, **e e e**.

Impy Ink says, **i i i**.

Oscar Orange says, **o o o**.

Uppy Umbrella says, **u u u**.

46

# Focus on sound

Draw lines to join the pictures to the right word.

egg

under

on

ink

ant

Whose sound starts each word? Circle the right one.

   a  e

   u  e

  i  o

  a  o

  i  u

# Focus on sound

Say Annie Apple's sound.    Say Eddy Elephant's sound.

Look at these pictures. Whose sound can you hear in the **middle** of each word? Write in the missing letter.

m_n

p_n

h_t

b_d

# Focus on sound

Say Impy Ink's sound.     Say Eddy Elephant's sound.

Look at these pictures. Whose sound can you hear in the **middle** of each word? Write in the missing letter.

w_n

t_n

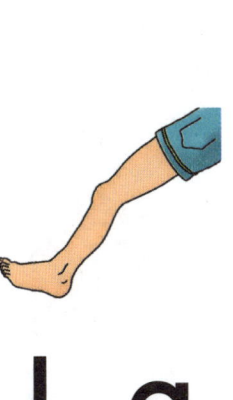
l_g

k_ck

# Focus on sound

Say Oscar Orange's sound.     Say Uppy Umbrella's sound.

Look at these pictures. Whose sound can you hear in the **middle** of each word? Circle the correct word.

hot   hut       hot   hut

dog   dug       jug   jog

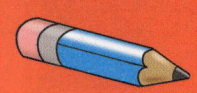
# Focus on sound

Say Annie Apple's sound.  Say Uppy Umbrella's sound.

Look at these pictures. Whose sound can you hear in the **middle** of each word? Circle the correct word.

bug    bag

bug    bag

hut    hat

sun    san

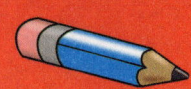
# Short vowels

Circle the word that matches the picture.

**bed**   **bus**   **bag**

**sun**   **six**   **sat**

**dig**   **dug**   **dog**

**cat**   **cup**   **cap**

# Short vowels

Read the words and draw the pictures in the boxes.

| | |
|---|---|
| big bed | six hats |
| red cup | hot sun |

# Focus on sound

Find Mr A's objects. Then colour the picture.

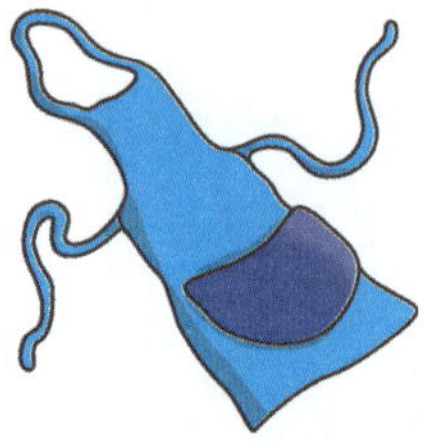

apron     alien

 # Shapes and sounds

 Copy Annie Apple's words into this box.

 Copy Mr A's words into this box.

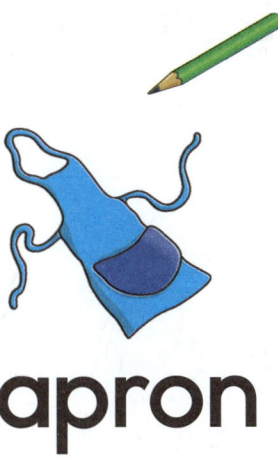
**apron**

**apple**

**alien**

**ant**

# Focus on sound

Find Mr E's objects. Then colour the picture.

east

east    eat

# Shapes and sounds

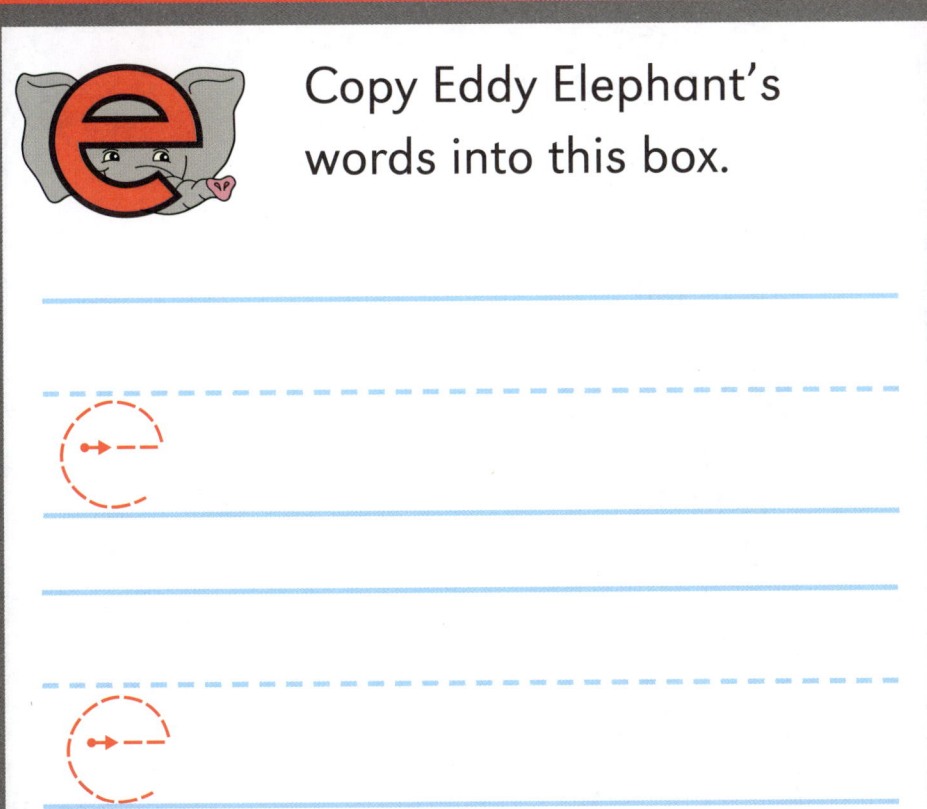

Copy Eddy Elephant's words into this box.

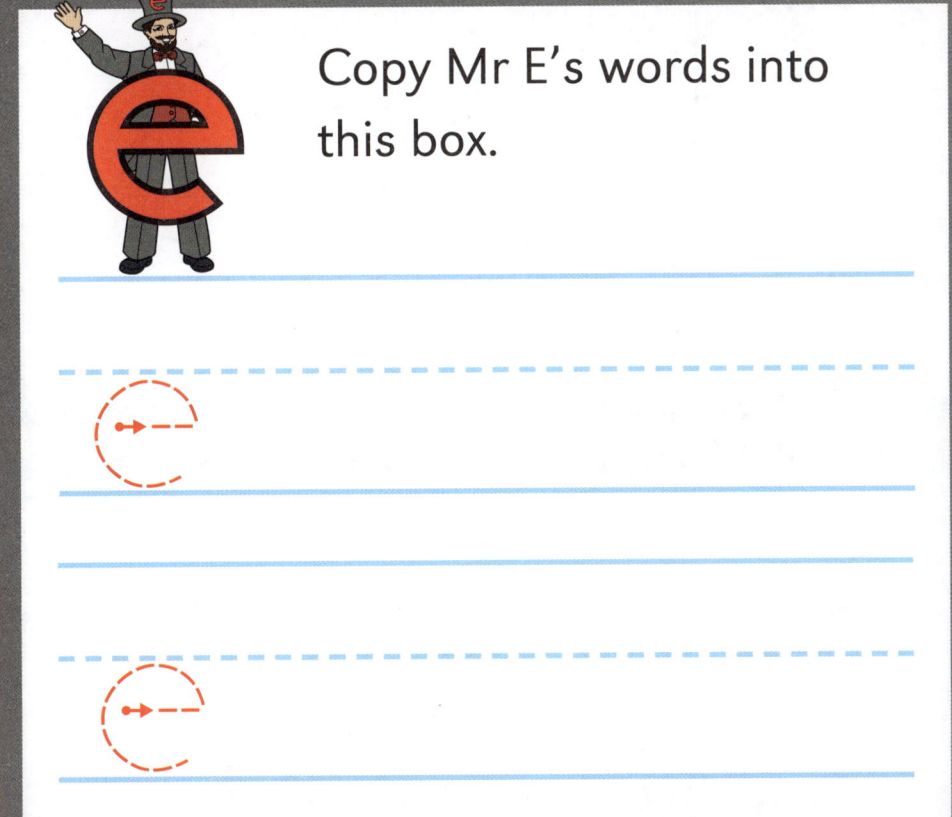

Copy Mr E's words into this box.

east

egg

elbow

eat

 Focus on sound

Find Mr I's objects. Then colour the picture.

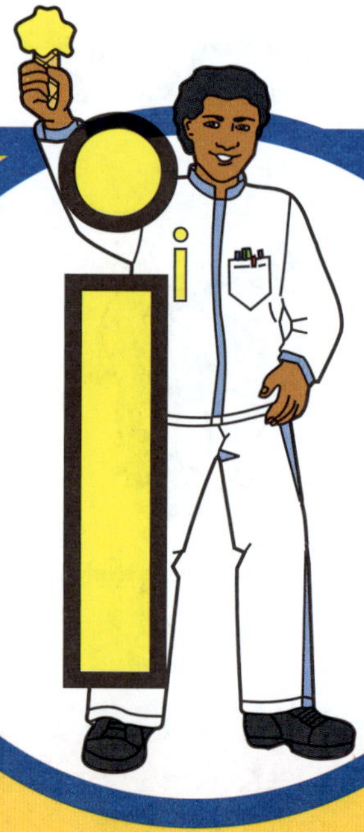

ice cream

island

# Shapes and sounds

Copy Impy Ink's words into this box.

Copy Mr I's words into this box.

ink

ice cream

island

insect

# Focus on sound

Find Mr O's objects. Then colour the picture.

old 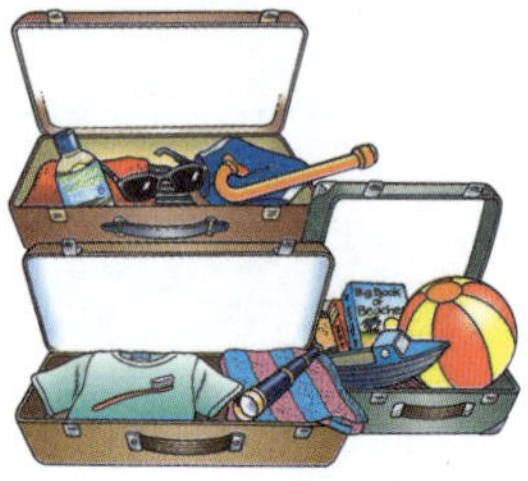   open

# Shapes and sounds

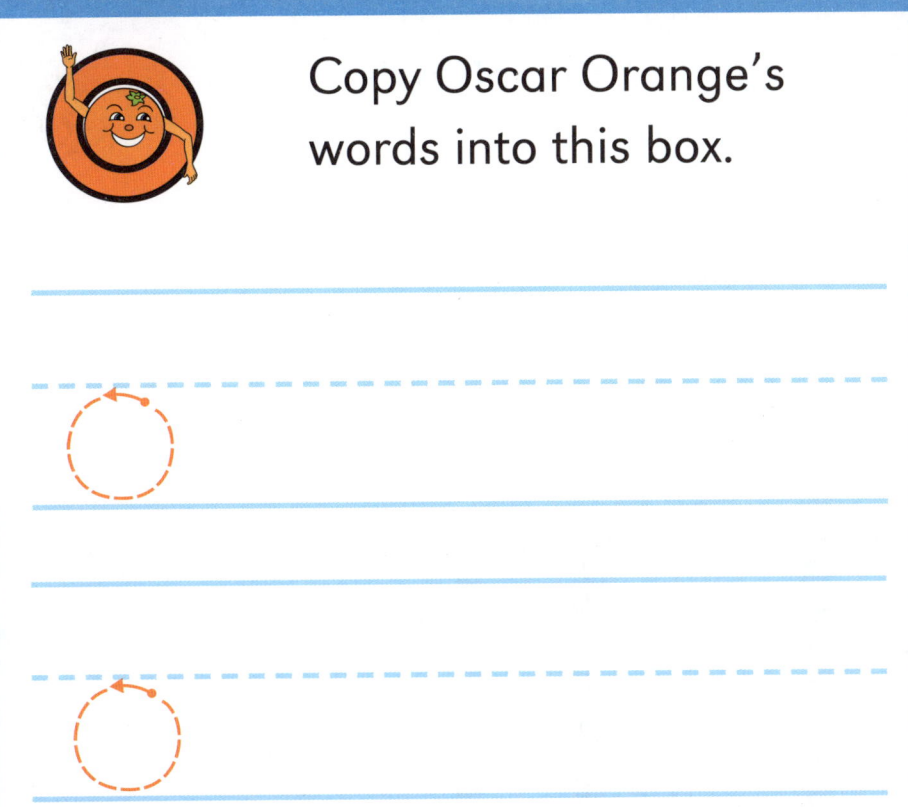

Copy Oscar Orange's words into this box.

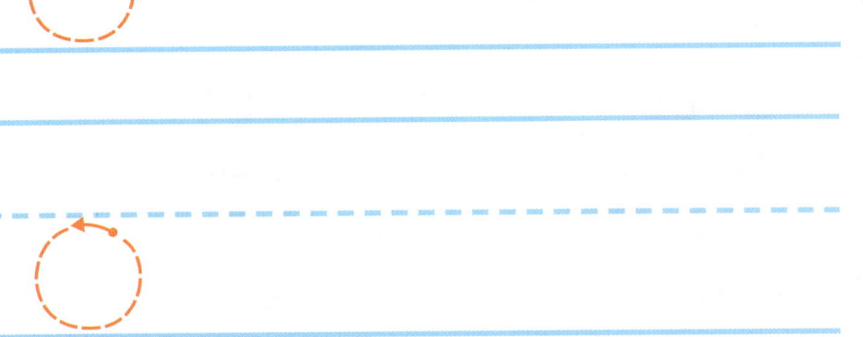

Copy Mr O's words into this box.

orange

open

on

old

# Focus on sound

Find Mr U's objects. Then colour the picture.

uniform   unicycle

# Shapes and sounds

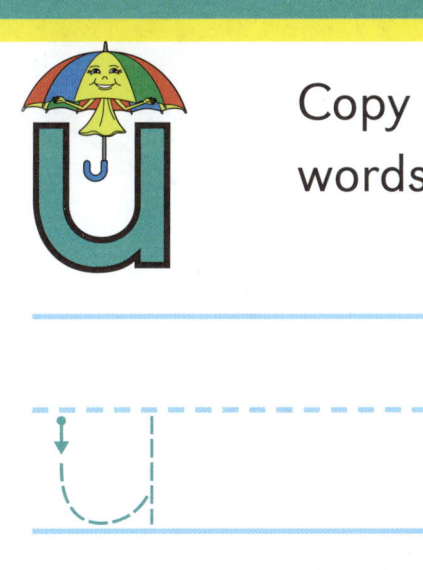

Copy Uppy Umbrella's words into this box.

Copy Mr U's words into this box.

uniform

under

up

unicycle

63

# Focus on sound

Look at these pictures. Who can you hear at the **beginning** of each word? Tick the correct box.

 ant  ☐  ☐

 eat  ☐  ☐

 insect  ☐ 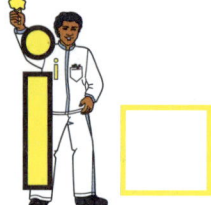 ☐

 on  ☐  ☐

 unicycle  ☐  ☐

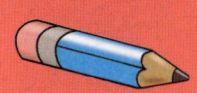
# Focus on sound

Look at these pictures. Who can you hear in the **middle** of each word? Tick the correct box.

 cake  ☐  ☐

 jet  ☐  ☐

 bike  ☐  ☐

 hot  ☐  ☐

 cup  ☐  ☐

65

# Rhyming words

Circle the words that do not rhyme in each row.

dog     log     bag     frog

sun     run     bun     bus

cat     hut     hat     bat

men     pen     hen     key

# Phonic Word Builder

Follow the path from Bouncy Ben. Write each letter on the line as you pass it. Then colour the shape.

The hidden word is __ __ __ __

# Blend the sounds

Match the objects to the correct Letterlanders. The first one has been done for you.

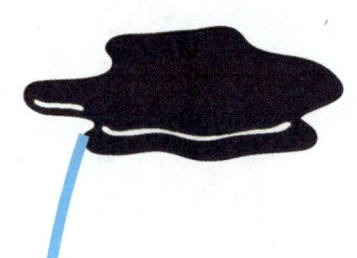
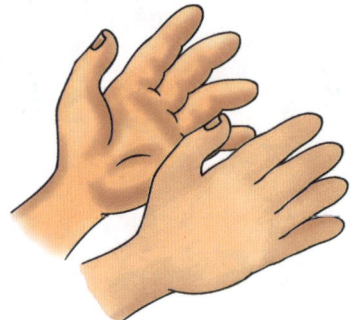
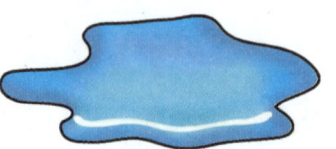

Can you think of any more words that start with these sounds?

# Blend the sounds

Write the correct letter shapes to finish the words.

 _____own

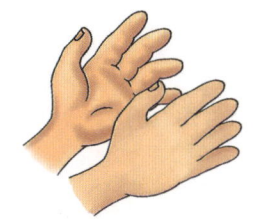 _____ap

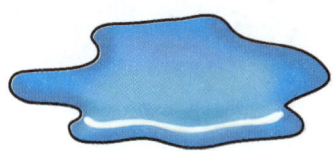 _____ue

 _____ock

_____ack

69

# Blend the sounds

Match the objects to the correct Letterlanders. The first one has been done for you.

Can you think of any more words that start with these sounds?

# Blend the sounds

Write the correct letter shapes to finish the words.

    \_\_\_\_ag

    \_\_\_\_oves

    \_\_\_\_owers

    \_\_\_\_ass

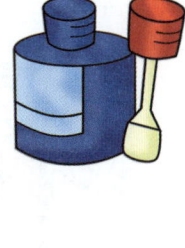    \_\_\_\_ue

    \_\_\_\_ame

# Blend the sounds

Match the objects to the correct Letterlanders. The first one has been done for you.

Can you think of any more words that start with these sounds?

# Blend the sounds

Write the correct letter shapes to finish the words.

 _____ant

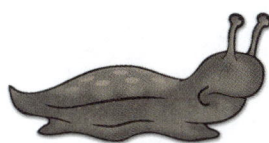 _____ug

 _____eep

 _____ate

 _____ide

 _____ug

# Blend the sounds

Match the objects to the correct Letterlanders. The first one has been done for you.

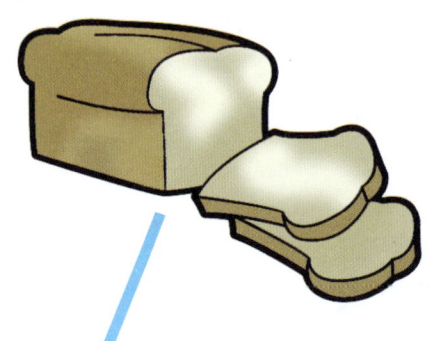
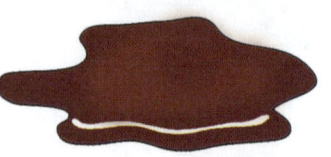

Can you think of any more words that start with these sounds?

# Blend the sounds

Write the correct letter shapes to finish the words.

\_\_\_\_own

\_\_\_\_icks

\_\_\_\_y

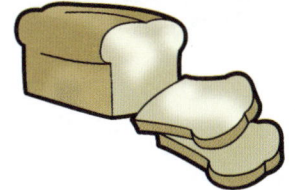
\_\_\_\_ead

\_\_\_\_ab

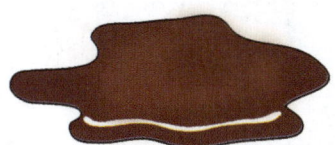
\_\_\_\_own

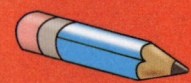

# Blend the sounds

Match the objects to the correct Letterlanders.
The first one has been done for you.

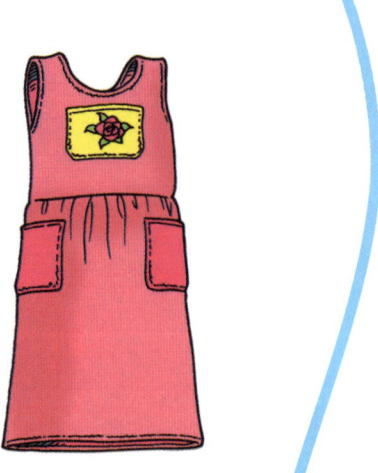

Can you think of any more words that start with these sounds?

# Blend the sounds

Write the correct letter shapes to finish the words.

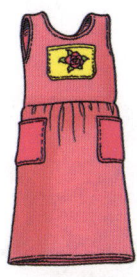 _____ess

 _____uit

 _____og

 _____um

 _____iends

 _____ink

# Blend the sounds

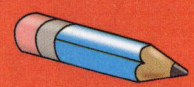

Match the objects to the correct Letterlanders. The first one has been done for you.

Can you think of any more words that start with these sounds?

# Blend the sounds

Write the correct letter shapes to finish the words.

 _____esent

 _____ass

 _____apes

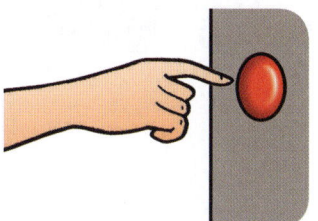 _____ess

 _____ice

 _____een

# Blend the sounds

Match the objects to the correct Letterlanders. The first one has been done for you.

Can you think of any more words that start with these sounds?

80

# Blend the sounds

Write the correct letter shapes to finish the words.

   _____ee

   _____uit

   _____og

   _____iangle

   _____ain

   _____iends

# Blend the sounds

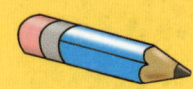

Match the objects to the correct Letterlanders. The first one has been done for you.

Can you think of any more words that start with these sounds?

# Blend the sounds

Write the correct letter shapes to finish the words.

    ____arf

    ____i

    ____irt

    ____ip

    ____hool

    ____ales

# Blend the sounds

Match the objects to the correct Letterlanders.
The first one has been done for you.

Can you think of any more words that start with these sounds?

84

# Blend the sounds

Write the correct letter shapes to finish the words.

_____amp

_____oon

_____op

_____ar

_____ace

_____in

# Blend the sounds

Match the objects to the correct Letterlanders.
The first one has been done for you.

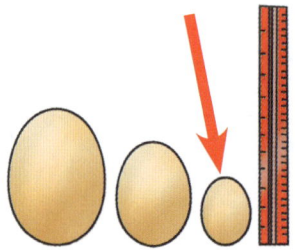

Can you think of any more words that start with these sounds?

 # Blend the sounds

Write the correct letter shapes to finish the words.

 _____ow

 _____ail

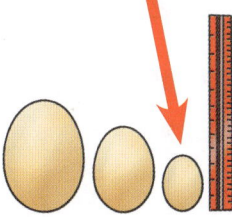 _____all

 _____ell

 _____ake

 _____ile

# Blend the sounds

Match the objects to the correct Letterlanders.
The first one has been done for you.

Can you think of any more words that start with these sounds?

Write the correct letter shapes to finish the words.

   ____im

   ____eet

# Let's review

Write the correct letters on the lines to finish these words.

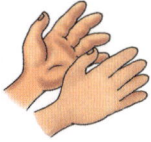 _ _ ap

 _ _ ag

 _ _ ant

 _ _ ug

 _ _ ick

 _ _ ab

 _ _ um

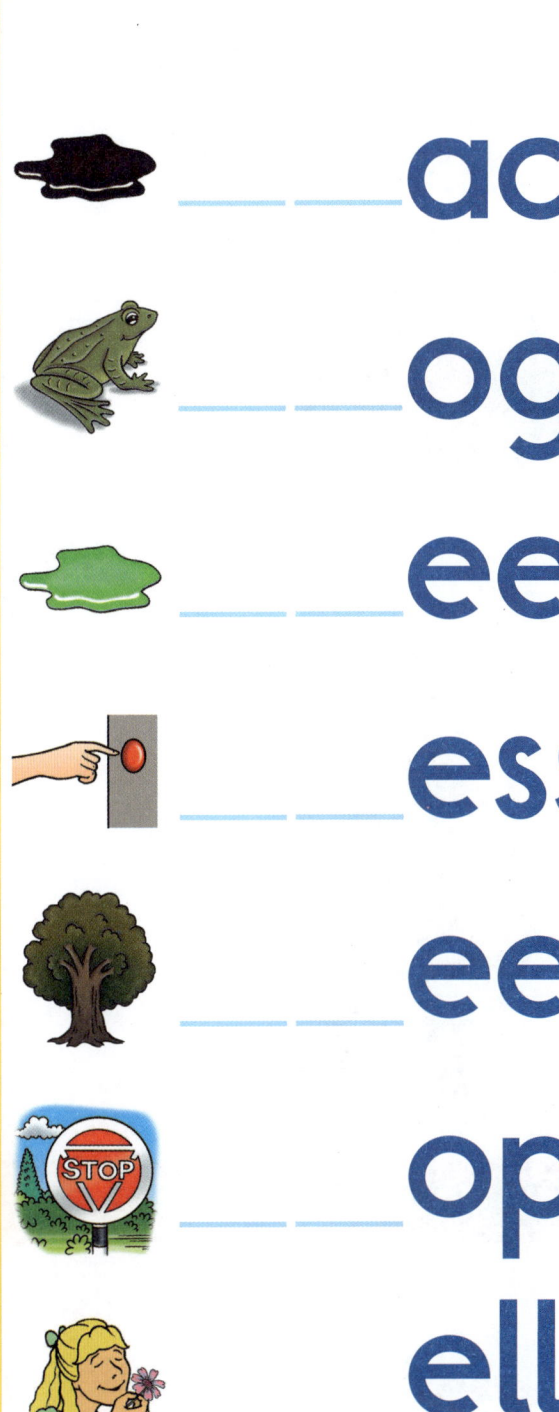

# Let's review

Draw lines to join Annie Apple and Mr A to the things that start with their sounds.

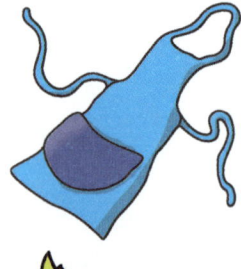

Whose sound does **ant** start with? Put a tick in the correct box.

ant

# Let's review

What is Bouncy Ben doing? Write Ben's letter on the lines to finish the sentence below.

__ouncy __en __ounces out of __ed.

Draw lines to join Clever Cat's words to the matching pictures.

cup     car     cat

# Let's review

**Dippy Duck loves to draw. Colour all the shapes with a 'd' in them to see what Dippy has drawn.**

It's a ___ ___ ___ ___ ___ .

# Let's review

Draw lines to join Eddy Elephant and Mr E to the things that start with their sounds.

Whose sound does **elbow** start with? Put a tick in the correct box.

elbow

93

# Let's review

Firefighter Fred has a fire to fight! Follow the paths to help him find the fire.

a
b
c

Which path did Fred need to take? Write the letter in the box.

94

# Let's review

Join the dots to finish the picture, beginning with a, b, c. Then colour it in.

It's my go-cart!

What did you find? Tick the correct box.

go-cart

guitar

# Let's review

Draw lines to join the round pictures to their place in the big picture of Harry Hat Man's hat shop.

# Let's review

Draw lines to join Impy Ink and Mr I to the things that start with their sounds.

Whose sound does **island** start with? Put a tick in the correct box.

island

 ☐    ☐

97

# Let's review

Draw a circle around each of Jumping Jim's jam jars that have a 'j' in them.

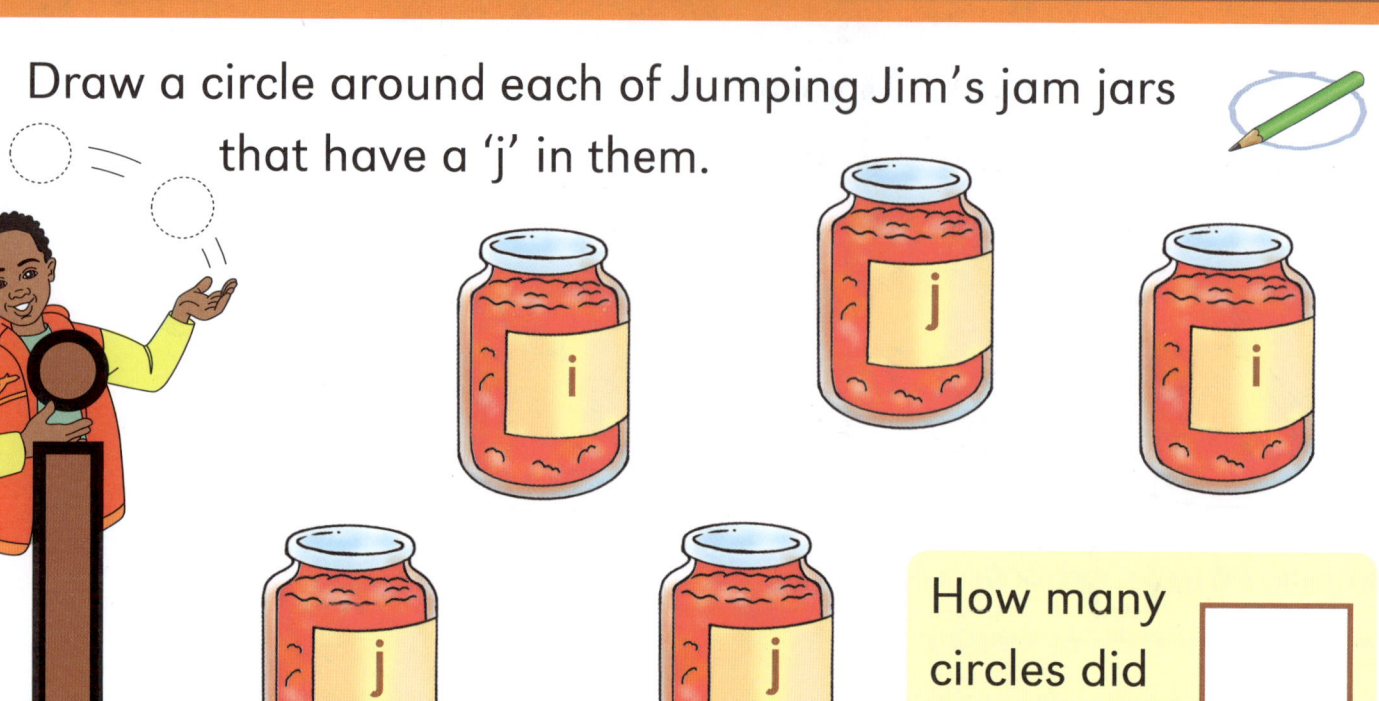

How many circles did you draw?

Kicking King is thinking about things that begin with his letter shape. Draw two things he could be thinking about.

# Let's review

Follow the lines to join the pictures to the words. Then trace over each word.

Lucy

lamp

log

Now make your own pattern, starting at the red dot.

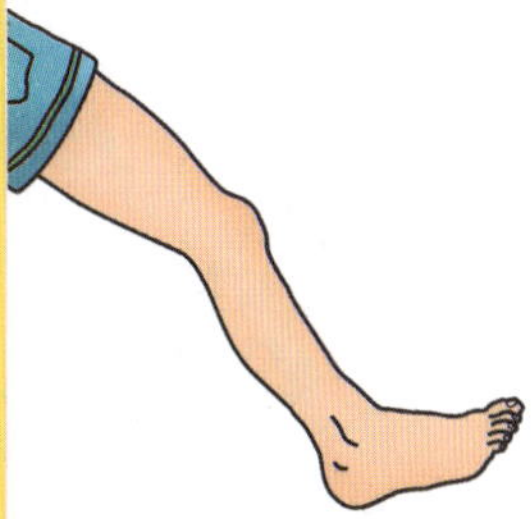

leg

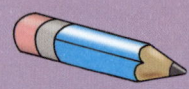

# Let's review

Can you see all the things that start with Munching Mike's sound? Finish colouring the picture.

Here's another word that starts with my sound. Finish writing it on the lines.

# Let's review

Noisy Nick's favourite number is nine. How many bowls of noodles can you count?

Draw more nuts so that there are nine altogether.

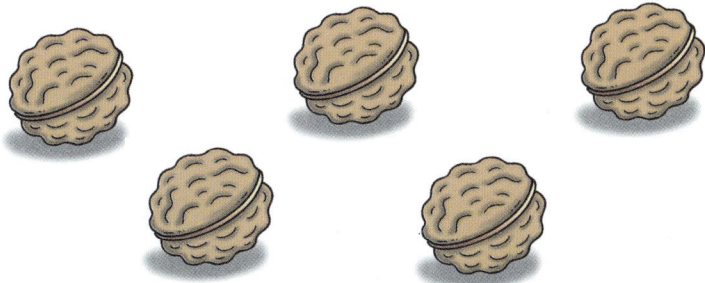

Draw a circle around the group with nine in it.

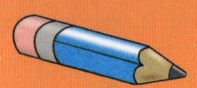# Let's review

Draw lines to join Oscar Orange and Mr O to the things that start with their sounds.

Whose sound does **orange** start with? Put a tick in the correct box.

**off**

 ☐   ☐

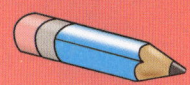

# Let's review

What is Peter Puppy doing? Write Peter's letter on the lines to finish the sentence below.

__eter __u___y __acks a __icnic.

Colour the quilts that have Quarrelsome Queen's letter in them.

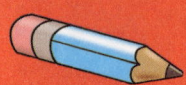

# Let's review

Can you see these things that start with Red Robot's sound? Tick the box as you find each one.

rain ☐

river ☐

rice ☐

rainbow ☐

Here's another word that starts with my sound. Trace over the letters.

rabbit

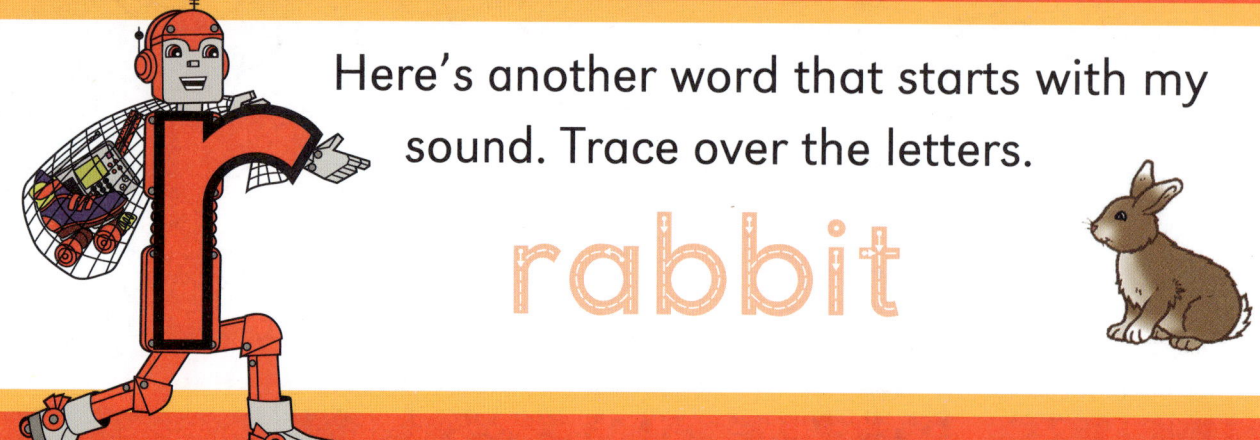

# Let's review

Sammy Snake likes to swim. Help him find his way to the other side.

Sammy Snake likes to

_____ _____ _____ _____ _____ .

# Let's review

In the grid below are words starting with Talking Tess's sound. Colour a star for each word you find.

```
t  l  t  r  e  e  q
e  m  p  a  o  t  e
n  r  c  a  v  m  u
z  t  e  d  d  y  t
t  r  a  i  n  p  h
```

  tree
  ten
 teddy
  train

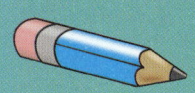
# Let's review

Draw lines to join Uppy Umbrella and Mr U to the things that start with their sounds.

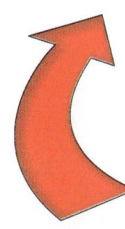

Whose sound does **uniform** start with? Put a tick in the correct box.

uniform

107

# Let's review

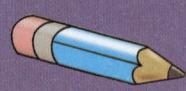

Follow the lines to join each picture to the right word. Then trace over the word.

Vicky

van

violin

Now make your own pattern, starting at the red dot.

vet

# Let's review

Draw lines to join the round pictures to their place in the big picture of Walter Walrus.

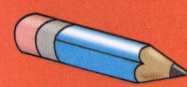
# Let's review

Fix-it Max's favourite number is six. How many tool boxes can you count?

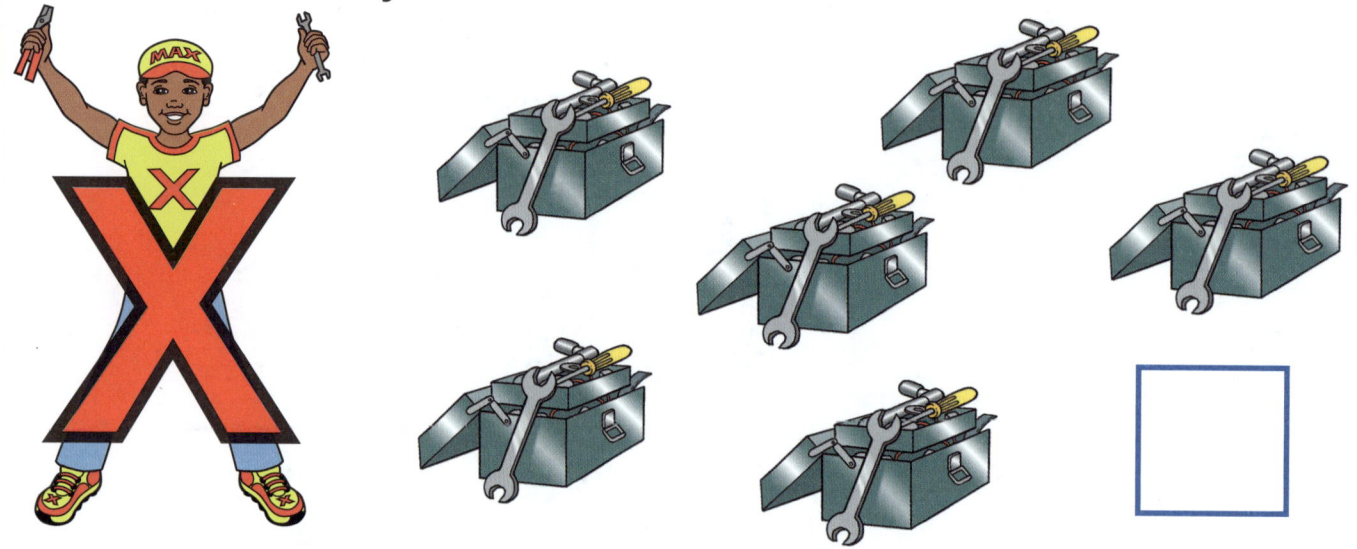

Draw more boxes so that there are six altogether.

Draw a circle around six foxes.

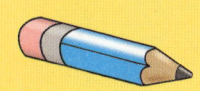

# Let's review

Draw a circle around each of Yellow Yo-yo Man's yo-yo's that have a 'y' in them.

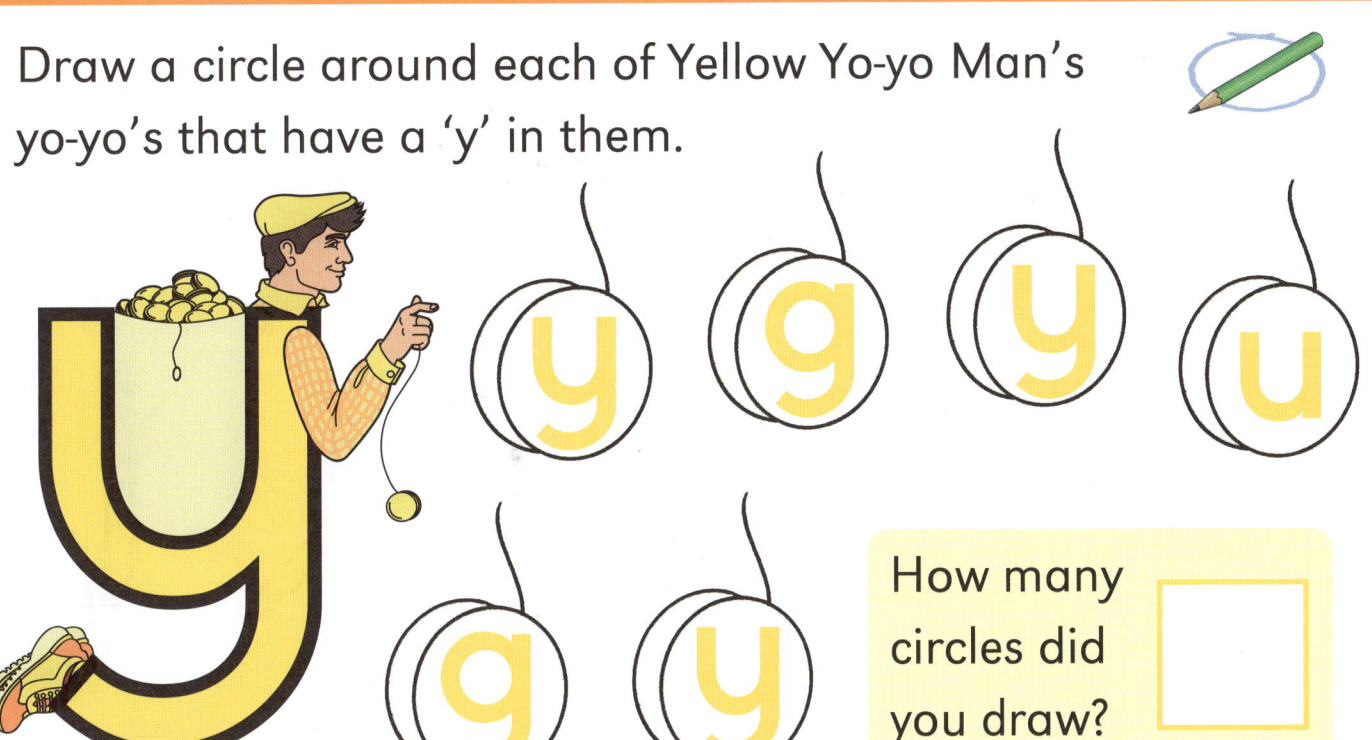

How many circles did you draw?

Where does Zig Zag Zebra live? Write Zig Zag's letter on the lines to finish the sentence below.

_ig _ag

_ebra lives

at the _oo.

# Letterland

Annie Apple    Bouncy Ben    Clever Cat    Dippy Duck    Eddy Elephant    Firefighter Fred

Golden Girl    Harry Hat Man    Impy Ink    Jumping Jim    Kicking King    Lucy Lamp Light

Munching Mike    Noisy Nick    Oscar Orange    Peter Puppy    Quarrelsome Queen    Red Robot    Sammy Snake

Talking Tess    Uppy Umbrella    Vicky Violet    Walter Walrus    Fix-it Max    Yellow Yo-yo Man    Zig Zag Zebra

Mr A    Mr E    Mr I    Mr O    Mr U